Rescues in Focus

Fire Rescues

by Mark L. Lewis

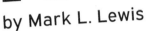

FOCUS READERS
BEACON

www.focusreaders.com

Focus Readers is distributed by North Star Editions:
sales@northstareditions.com | 888-417-0195

Produced for Focus Readers by Red Line Editorial.

Photographs ©: Praisaeng/Shutterstock Images, cover, 1; VCNW/Shutterstock Images, 4; Tony_ Bendele/iStockphoto, 7; rkl_foto/Shutterstock Images, 9; asiseeit/iStockphoto, 10; SrA Alexa Culbert/ U.S. Air Force/AB Forces News Collection/Alamy, 13, 29; Bob Shanley/Palm Beach Post/Zuma Press/ Newscom, 15; Marsan/Shutterstock Images, 17; Christian Roberts-Olsen/Shutterstock Images, 18–19; simonkr/iStockphoto, 20; LightField Studios/Shutterstock Images, 23; gorodenkoff/iStockphoto, 25; Sgt. Stephanie Ramirez/US Army Reserve/Defense Visual Information Distribution Service, 27 (firefighter); Jaanta/Shutterstock Images, 27 (air tank); Ralf Geithe/iStockphoto, 27 (ladder)

Library of Congress Cataloging-in-Publication Data
Names: Lewis, Mark L., 1991- author.
Title: Fire rescues / by Mark L. Lewis.
Description: Lake Elmo, MN : Focus Readers, [2020] | Series: Rescues in focus |
  Audience: Grade 4 to 6. | Includes bibliographical references and index.
Identifiers: LCCN 2018058104 (print) | LCCN 2018060029 (ebook) | ISBN
  9781641859790 (PDF) | ISBN 9781641859103 (ebook) | ISBN 9781641857727
  (hardcover) | ISBN 9781641858410 (pbk.)
Subjects: LCSH: Lifesaving at fires--Juvenile literature.
Classification: LCC TH9402 (ebook) | LCC TH9402 .L49 2020 (print) | DDC
  628.9/2--dc23
LC record available at https://lccn.loc.gov/2018058104

Printed in the United States of America
Mankato, MN
May, 2019

About the Author

Mark L. Lewis lives in Minnesota but has traveled all over the world. He loves writing books for young readers.

Table of Contents

Chapter 1

House Fire

Firefighters received a call in Cocoa, Florida. A house was on fire. Someone was trapped inside. The firefighters knew they had to act fast. Fires can spread through a house in just a few minutes.

A fire can occur in any house.

Two young boys stood outside the house. They had been inside. A neighbor had helped them get out. Now, the boys pointed at the house. Their grandmother was still inside. Most of the house was on fire. But the grandmother's bedroom was not.

Did You Know?

On average, more than 350,000 house fires happen every year in the United States.

 Many firefighters are often needed to rescue victims and put out the fire.

Matt Holladay was one of the firefighters there. Holladay asked another firefighter to stand by the bedroom window. Smoke had filled the room. This made it hard to see.

Holladay told the other firefighter to yell if it was hard to find the exit. That way, Holladay could follow the firefighter's voice.

Holladay climbed through the window. He landed near the grandmother. He felt his way along the floor to reach her. Her eyes were open. But she didn't say anything. Holladay passed her to his teammates.

Another firefighter felt the grandmother's **pulse**. She was alive.

 A house may not be safe to enter even after the fire is out.

She needed to go straight to the hospital. But she was going to be okay. The house was destroyed. But thanks to the rescuers, no one was seriously hurt.

Chapter 2

Becoming a Firefighter

There are several ways to become a firefighter. Some people study fire science in college. Other people go to fire **academies**. These schools train future firefighters. Fire academy lasts 12 to 14 weeks.

 Firefighters train with a fire truck and hose at their fire academy.

Recruits train for eight to ten hours per day. In total, they must finish 600 hours of training.

Drills are a major part of fire academy. In each drill, recruits practice a specific firefighting task. For example, recruits practice using hoses. They also practice putting on their gear. Firefighting gear can be heavy. Firefighters have to put it on quickly. Someone's life may depend on how fast firefighters can reach the house.

 Firefighters learn to drag a victim by crossing their arms around the dummy's chest.

Firefighters also practice carrying dummies out of buildings. Dummies weigh the same as an adult person.

Dummies also do not move. A dummy **simulates** a person who is unconscious. Using dummies teaches firefighters how to move a person safely. Many firefighters also receive medical training. Helping hurt people is a key part of the job.

Some drills are in places known as burn buildings. Burn buildings

 Sometimes firefighters use a deserted building to act as their burn building.

are made specifically for training. First, a seasoned firefighter sets the burn building on fire. Then, recruits practice putting it out. These drills are safer ways to work with fire.

Wildland firefighters get the same training as city firefighters. But they also learn about forests and wildfires. These firefighters practice **navigating** different surroundings. They train to use ropes, too. Ropes help when someone is hard to reach.

Did You Know?

Wildland firefighters are known as hotshots. They got this name from working in the hottest part of the fire.

If a fire victim is unable to move, rescuers might use ropes to get him or her to safety.

Not all firefighters go to fire academy. Some people volunteer. These firefighters work without pay. Every path to become a firefighter is difficult. But with the right training, firefighters can save lives.

Trapped in the Mountains

In October 2018, a fire broke out in Nevada. It burned through the Ruby Mountains. Flames shot 100 feet (30 m) into the air. **Embers** blew all over.

Nine people were on top of one of the canyons. They tried to escape the fire. However, boulders had fallen in their way. Everyone was trapped.

Soon, rescuers arrived in large water trucks. First, they cleared the road. Then, they worked to control the fire. With the path cleared, all nine people made it to safety.

Most wildfires in the United States are caused by people.

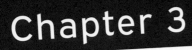

Chapter 3

On the Job

Firefighters act quickly when a call comes in. First, the firefighters get dressed. They put on heavy boots and suits. These items protect them from flames. Then, firefighters put on air tanks.

Gas masks protect firefighters from smoke and connect to their air tanks.

That is because burning buildings are filled with smoke. Breathing in the smoke is unsafe. Air tanks help firefighters breathe clean air.

Next, the firefighters board the fire truck. Important tools are in the truck. They include hoses, ladders, and axes. The firefighters drive to the fire as quickly as possible.

At the fire, firefighters go to work. Some firefighters connect hoses to fire **hydrants**. The hoses carry water from the hydrants to the fire.

 Most fire hoses are 50 feet (15 m) long.

Other firefighters set up ladders. The firefighters must figure out where the fire is worst. They may use the ladder to study the fire. But first, they check for people inside. If people are trapped, the firefighters try to rescue them.

Some firefighters go inside. They knock down doors with axes. Other firefighters stay outside. They guide the firefighters who are inside. This method helps keep firefighters safe when **visibility** is low.

Inside, the firefighters find the people who are trapped. They bring them out of the building.

Did You Know?

Approximately half of all house fires start in the kitchen.

 A fire can make a house as hot as 600 degrees Fahrenheit (316°C).

Then, they check to make sure the victims are okay. Firefighters are trained as **paramedics**. They treat small injuries and help **stabilize** the victims. They often ride with people to the hospital.

Wildland firefighters mainly try to stop fires from reaching anyone's house. But these firefighters sometimes still need to rescue people. A hiker may get stuck at the bottom of a cliff. The firefighters go to the cliff above the hiker. They tie ropes around something sturdy, such as a tree. Next, they

Did You Know?

Wildland firefighters sometimes rescue animals that are trapped in fires.

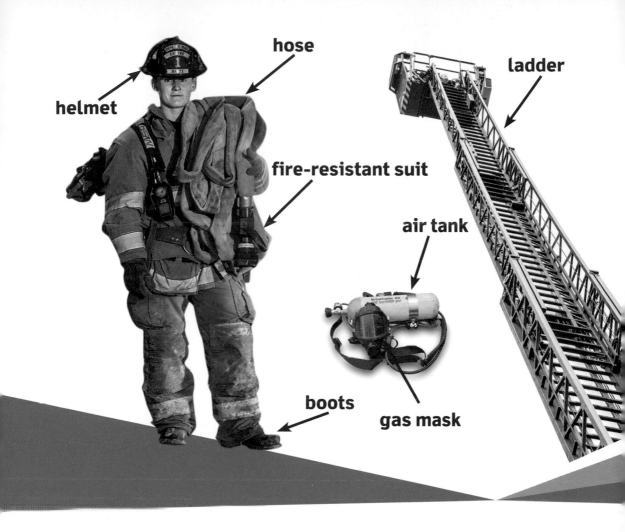

helmet

hose

ladder

fire-resistant suit

air tank

boots

gas mask

drop the ropes from the top of the cliff. A firefighter climbs down to the person. Then, the firefighter moves the person to safety.

FOCUS ON
Fire Rescues

Write your answers on a separate piece of paper.

1. Write a sentence describing the main idea of Chapter 2.

2. If you were a firefighter, would you rather put out building fires or wildfires? Why?

3. Which piece of equipment connects to a fire hydrant?
   A. axe
   B. hose
   C. air tank

4. Why do some firefighters stay outside when putting out a fire?
   A. They are too afraid to go inside the building.
   B. They do not have the correct gear to fight fires.
   C. They give directions to the firefighters inside.

5. What does **unconscious** mean in this book?

*Dummies also do not move. A dummy simulates a person who is **unconscious**.*

    A. not real

    B. not awake

    C. not smart

6. What does **seasoned** mean in this book?

*First, a **seasoned** firefighter sets the burn building on fire. Then, recruits practice putting it out.*

    A. trained and experienced

    B. new and unskilled

    C. retired and volunteer

Answer key on page 32.

Glossary

academies
Schools for special skills.

embers
Small pieces of burning wood in a fire.

hydrants
Large pipes in the street that firefighters can draw water from.

navigating
Finding one's way while traveling.

paramedics
Medical professionals who help during emergencies.

pulse
The movement of blood in the body.

recruits
New members of a group.

simulates
Creates an imitation of something.

stabilize
To stop someone's health from declining.

visibility
The ability to see or be seen.

To Learn More

BOOKS

McKinney, Devon. *A Firefighter's Tools*. New York: PowerKids Press, 2016.

Thiessen, Mark. *Extreme Wildfire: Smoke Jumpers, High-Tech Gear, Survival Tactics, and the Extraordinary Science of Fire*. Washington, DC: National Geographic, 2016.

Waeschle, Amy. *Daring Wildfire Rescues*. North Mankato, MN: Capstone Press, 2018.

NOTE TO EDUCATORS

Visit **www.focusreaders.com** to find lesson plans, activities, links, and other resources related to this title.

Index

NEW JERSEY DEVILS

BY LUKE HANLON

Book design by Maggie Villaume
Cover design by Maggie Villaume

Photographs ©: Bill Kostroun/AP Images, cover, 16–17, 18, 23, 27; Karl B. DeBlaker/AP Images, 4–5; Frank Franklin II/AP Images, 6, 8; Ray Stubblebine/AP Images, 10–11; Liu Heung Shing/AP Images, 12; Bob Kostroun/AP Images, 15; Ryan Remiorz/Canadian Press/AP Images, 21; Gregory Smith/AP Images, 24–25; Del Mecum/Cal Sport Media/AP Images, 29

Press Box Books, an imprint of Press Room Editions.

ISBN
978-1-63494-677-3 (library bound)
978-1-63494-701-5 (paperback)
978-1-63494-747-3 (epub)
978-1-63494-725-1 (hosted ebook)

Library of Congress Control Number: 2022919588

Distributed by North Star Editions, Inc.
2297 Waters Drive
Mendota Heights, MN 55120
www.northstareditions.com

Printed in the United States of America
082023

ABOUT THE AUTHOR
Luke Hanlon is a sportswriter and editor based in Minneapolis.

TABLE OF CONTENTS

1

Hughes's first career assist in 2019 made him the third-youngest player to record a point in team history.

BROTHERLY
LOVE

The New Jersey Devils were one of the worst teams in the National Hockey League (NHL) in the 2018–19 season. They missed the playoffs for the sixth time in seven years. However, all of that losing helped the Devils get the top pick in the 2019 NHL Draft. They used it on center Jack Hughes.

Hughes was only 18 years old. But the Devils put him in the

Quinn (right) and Jack Hughes (left) talk during a 2019 game.

lineup right away for his debut season in 2019–20. It took Hughes some time to adjust to the new league. The Devils also struggled, losing their first six games. Then, in the seventh game, Hughes recorded his first assist. It helped the Devils earn their first win.

Two days later, Hughes made an even bigger impact. The Devils were hosting the Vancouver Canucks and Hughes's older brother, Quinn. Their parents were watching and cheering from the stands.

The Devils went on a power play late in the first period. Left winger Taylor Hall skated around a Vancouver defender. It looked like he had a chance to shoot. Instead, he slid a perfect pass across

Jack Hughes (right) celebrates his first career NHL goal in 2019.

the ice. The pass caught the Canucks off guard.

Hughes needed only a moment to control the puck. The center unleashed a hard wrist shot from near the faceoff circle. It found the back of the net for his first NHL goal. Hughes's tally proved to be the game winner. The Devils beat the Canucks 1–0. Hughes went on to put up 21 points in his rookie season. The young talent was already making himself known around the NHL. And the fans in New Jersey knew they had a star in the making.

FAMILY HAT TRICK

Quinn Hughes reached the NHL in 2019. Jack Hughes followed later that year. But the family wasn't done with those two. In 2021, the Devils drafted their younger brother Luke Hughes. All three were first-round draft picks. That was a first for a trio of US-born brothers.

2

Dennis Patterson (left) reacts after the Kansas City Scouts gave up another goal in an 8–2 loss to the New York Rangers in 1975.

SETTLING IN JERSEY

The Devils played their first season far away from New Jersey. They started as the Kansas City Scouts in 1974. But the franchise got off to a rough start. The Scouts won 27 of 160 games in their first two seasons. Fans lost interest in a hurry. The team then moved to Denver and became the Colorado Rockies.

Things didn't get any better in Colorado. So after the 1981–82

New Jersey Devils goalie Ron Low saves a shot from Los Angeles Kings center Marcel Dionne in 1984.

season, a new owner bought the team with the intent to move it. John McMullen was a New Jersey native. He wanted his team to play there. So he settled the franchise in East Rutherford, New Jersey. The team needed a new name. McMullen put the decision to a fan vote, and they selected the Devils.

The name is a reference to the Jersey Devil. The legendary creature has the body and head of a horse but wings like a bat. Legend has it that the Jersey Devil lives in the forests of the Garden State.

MICKEY MOUSE

The Devils lost 13–4 against the Edmonton Oilers in a 1983 game. Afterward, Oilers star Wayne Gretzky said the Devils were "putting a Mickey Mouse operation on the ice." The Oilers returned to New Jersey two months later. Devils fans wore Mickey Mouse ears in response to Gretzky.

The team had a fierce new name. But its play remained poor. The Devils never won more than 29 games in their first five seasons in New Jersey. So before the 1987–88 season, they hired Lou Lamoriello as team president. He proved to be the change New Jersey needed. Lamoriello's management went on to change the Devils forever.

The Devils made the playoffs in his first year in charge. They opened the playoffs by defeating the New York Islanders in six games. In the second round, New Jersey faced the Washington Capitals. In Game 7, John MacLean's third-period goal lifted the Devils to a 3–2 win. The Boston Bruins ended New

Though just 21 years old, goalie Sean Burke started 17 of the 20 games the Devils played in the 1988 playoffs. He ended up with a save percentage of .889.

Jersey's surprising run in Game 7 of the conference finals. But the Devils had finally arrived.

3

Martin Brodeur (right) and Scott Niedermayer defend the Devils' net in a 1999 game.

DEVILS DYNASTY

It took the New Jersey Devils 14 years and three cities to put together a winning season. But once the winning started, it didn't slow down. Starting in 1989–90, the Devils made the playoffs for six straight seasons. They suffered multiple first-round exits. But they got back to the conference finals in 1994. Waiting for them was their biggest rival, the New York Rangers.

Valeri Zelepukin (left) watches as his shot is saved in the first period of Game 3 in the 1994 Eastern Conference finals.

The back-and-forth series came down to Game 7. Playing at home, New York went up 1–0 in the second. The Devils desperately fought to answer. Finally, with 7.7 seconds left, left winger Valeri Zelepukin tied it. However, the Rangers eventually won in double overtime.

It was a heartbreaking way to end a season. But the Devils' roster remained strong. A 22-year-old Martin Brodeur was beginning his legendary goaltending career. Meanwhile, future Hall of Famers Scott Niedermayer and Scott Stevens anchored the blue line. Niedermayer was a calm leader, while Stevens brought huge hits.

In 1995, the Devils lost only four playoff games on their way to the Stanley Cup Final. They didn't let up against the Detroit Red Wings in the final series. Detroit featured a handful of future Hall of Famers. But the Devils core outplayed them. Two 5–2 home victories in a row sealed the 4–0 series sweep for New Jersey, and its very first championship.

The Devils missed the playoffs in 1995–96. But they started another playoff streak in the following season. This one lasted 13 years. The core of Brodeur, Niedermayer, and Stevens remained strong. And winger Patrik Elias was blossoming into a star.

The high-scoring Elias had a huge impact in the playoffs in 2000. His 13 assists were the most of any player in the postseason. The last one came on Jason Arnott's double-overtime goal in Game 6

CUP FOR A DAY

The 1994–95 Devils thought of a new way to celebrate a championship. Each player got a day with the Stanley Cup. Teams have followed that tradition ever since. Players often bring the Cup to their hometowns for celebrations. Parades and parties are common.

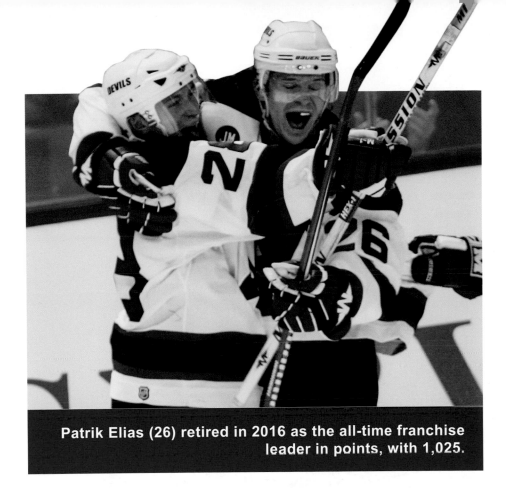

Patrik Elias (26) retired in 2016 as the all-time franchise leader in points, with 1,025.

of the Final against the Dallas Stars. That secured New Jersey's second title.

The Devils won a third title after shutting out the Mighty Ducks of Anaheim in Game 7 of the 2003 Final. With three Cups in nine years, the Devils were now among the NHL's best.

MARTIN BRODEUR

It's not hard to understand why fans consider Martin Brodeur one of the best goaltenders in history. Brodeur set NHL records with 1,266 games played, 691 wins, and 125 shutouts.

Brodeur did more than stop shots. He also set up his teammates for shots. Brodeur's 45 assists were tied for the third most by an NHL goalie when he retired. He also scored three goals during his career.

Brodeur was the backbone of the most successful era of Devils hockey. That started when he won the Calder Memorial Trophy in 1993–94. That award is given to the best rookie in the league. Brodeur went on to win four Vezina Trophies with the Devils. That goes to the best goaltender each season. Most importantly, he led New Jersey to three Stanley Cups.

Martin Brodeur celebrates as the Devils win the 1995 Stanley Cup Final over the Detroit Red Wings.

4

Patrik Elias went through the ups and downs with the Devils. His entire 20-year career was spent in New Jersey.

A NEW HOME

The New Jersey Devils continued to make the playoffs after their Cup win in 2003. In 2007–08, they also moved to the Prudential Center. The new home was about 20 minutes away in Newark, New Jersey.

Fans continued to see winning seasons. But the Devils' era of playoff dominance was over. They lost in the first two rounds for six straight seasons after their Cup win in 2003. In 2011, the Devils missed the playoffs entirely for the first time in 14 seasons.

It looked like the best days were behind the Devils. But they bounced back the next season. Patrik Elias was still dishing out assists. Ilya Kovalchuk, Zach Parise, and David Clarkson each scored 30 or more goals. And a 39-year-old Martin Brodeur was still a top goalie.

ONE AND ONLY

New Jersey is the home to many professional teams. But most are teams with New York in their names. The New York Giants, New York Jets, and New York Red Bulls all play in New Jersey. When the New Jersey Nets moved to Brooklyn in 2012, the Devils became the only professional team with New Jersey in its name.

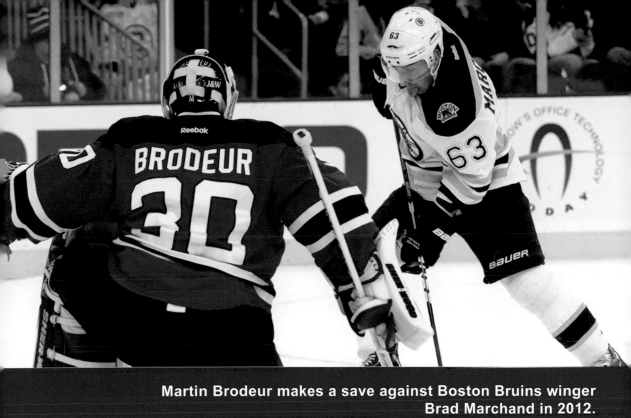

Martin Brodeur makes a save against Boston Bruins winger Brad Marchand in 2012.

Just as in 1994, the Devils met the New York Rangers in the 2012 conference finals. This series ended in six games. Devils center Adam Henrique scored in overtime to ignite the Prudential Center. The Devils headed back to the Cup Final. However, the Los Angeles Kings denied their quest for another championship.

The Devils' play declined after that. Parise left in 2012. Within four years, Kovalchuk, Brodeur, and Elias were all gone, too. Legend Lou Lamoriello stepped down in 2015. But then, the Devils traded for former first overall draft pick Taylor Hall. The winger tallied 93 points and won the Hart Memorial Trophy in 2017–18. That is given to the most valuable player in the league. The Devils were back in the playoffs for the first time in six years.

The success didn't last long. So the Devils started over with young talent. The 20-year-old Jack Hughes scored 26 goals in 2021–22. That tied 23-year-old Jesper Bratt for most on the team. Bratt also added 47 assists to lead the Devils that

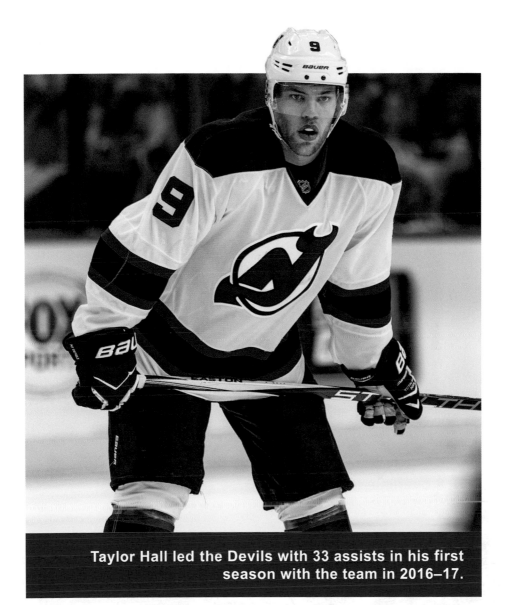

Taylor Hall led the Devils with 33 assists in his first season with the team in 2016–17.

season. Fans in New Jersey had hope that their new core of young stars could lead them back to the top.

• NEW JERSEY DEVILS
QUICK STATS

TEAM HISTORY: Kansas City Scouts (1974–76), Colorado Rockies (1976–82), New Jersey Devils (1982–)

STANLEY CUP CHAMPIONSHIPS: 3 (1995, 2000, 2003)

KEY COACHES:

- Jacques Lemaire (1993–98, 2009–11): 276 wins, 166 losses, 57 ties, 10 overtime losses

- Larry Robinson (1999–2002, 2005–06): 87 wins, 56 losses, 19 ties, 11 overtime losses

- Pat Burns (2002–04): 89 wins, 45 losses, 22 ties, 8 overtime losses

HOME ARENA: Prudential Center (Newark, NJ)

MOST CAREER POINTS: Patrik Elias (1,025)

MOST CAREER GOALS: Patrik Elias (408)

MOST CAREER ASSISTS: Patrik Elias (617)

MOST CAREER SHUTOUTS: Martin Brodeur (124)

*Stats are accurate through the 2021–22 season.

GLOSSARY

ASSIST
A pass, rebound, or deflection that results in a goal.

CONFERENCE
A smaller group of teams that make up a part of a sports league.

DEBUT
A player's first appearance for a team or league.

DRAFT
An event held every year where teams select new rookie players coming into the league.

RIVAL
An opposing player or team that brings out the greatest emotion from fans and players.

SWEEP
When a team wins all the games in a series.

TEAM PRESIDENT
The person in charge of all operations of a team.

• TO LEARN
MORE

BOOKS

Davidson, B. Keith. *NHL*. New York: Crabtree Publishing, 2022.

Doeden, Matt. *G.O.A.T. Hockey Teams*. Minneapolis: Lerner Publications, 2021.

Duling, Kaitlyn. *Women in Hockey*. Lake Elmo, MN: Focus Readers, 2020.

MORE INFORMATION

To learn more about the New Jersey Devils, go to **pressboxbooks.com/AllAccess**.

These links are routinely monitored and updated to provide the most current information available.

INDEX